Scream Savers

Calming Ideas for Frazzled Moms

by
Karol Ladd

PUBLISHING GROUP

Nashville, Tennessee

⭐ Scream Savers 💖

Calming Ideas for Frazzled Moms

Loaded down with laundry? Pooped out with preschoolers? Distracted with dinner? Frazzled with frustrations? Do you feel as though you want to scream? You are not alone. Every mother knows the feeling of mounting tensions when emotions take over and she wants to explode. Relax, this book was written to help you through those moments. Take a deep breath and relish the calming ideas in this valuable little tool for mothers. You will find ways to make your home a relaxing environment in the section labeled "Prescriptions for Peace." To help you through the heat of the moment you can refer to the "Keeping Your Cool" section. Perhaps you need creative, yet quiet, activities for the kids to provide a mood of silent serenity and solitude for mom. Flip over to Section Three for great ideas for "Quiet Activities with Kids." Finally, there are times when you need a few moments to yourself. How can you take a retreat in the midst of the your long list of responsibilities? Check out the "Mommy Moments" in Section Four! You will find new ideas to help you relax and find relief amidst the challenges of life.

This idea-packed book is not intended to solve all of your frustrations or relieve all your tensions. It is rather a book of assistance to help you deal with the moments of stress in a positive manner. You will feel better about yourself and maintain the respect of those around you when you are able to save a scream from ever leaving your lungs. The thoughts and helps herein will encourage a gentler and quieter spirit as you lovingly tend to the needs of your family each day. Relish and relax!

Contents

Prescriptions for PEACE

Prescriptions for
PEACE

1. Priority One

Life is hard. When you multiply the challenges in life by the amount of children for which you care, it can get down right difficult. Thankfully, we can go to the Maker of Life for instructions, directions, help and solace. The good news is that He wants to hear from you. Yes, God desires for you to come to Him to find peace and rest for your weary soul. Jesus said, "Come to Me, all you who labor and are heavy laden, and I will give you rest." Does that describe you? Are you heavy laden? Could you use a rest? Jesus opens the invitation to bring our lives to Him and lay our cares at His feet.

When is the last time you talked to Him? I mean prayed - not just the dinner table version. As caretakers of the precious little ones, prayer is an *essential* element of life. For what do you pray? Pray for wisdom in raising your kids to be Godly people of integrity and honor. Pray for their salvation, their safety, and their purity. Pray for the person they will marry one day. Pray for your God's strength to make it through each day with joy and peace. Set aside a little time each day to devote to prayer and reading the playbook (The Bible). When we consult the Creator and read the instructions, the game of life seems to play out a little differently than if we try to wing it on our own.

As parents searching for peace in the midst of life's storms, we can find our solace in the One who calms the sea. Although the Almighty may not change our circumstances, He is with us through our challenges, leading and guiding us with His calm assurance. The apostle Paul recognized the true source of inner peace as he wrote from a prison cell, "Do not be anxious about anything, but in everything, by prayer and petition, with thanksgiving, present your requests to God. And the peace of God, which transcends

1. Priority One

all understanding, will guard your hearts and your minds in Christ Jesus." So what is priority one? It's prayer. Pray about everything and experience the "peace which passes all understanding." Your kids are worth it!

Personal Notes:

_____

_____

_____

_____

_____

_____

_____

_____

_____

_____

_____

_____

_____

2. What Sends You?

Whining Kids? Messy House? Too many obligations? Sibling riots? The neighbor's kids? Continuous laundry? We all have our breaking point, and it is different for each of us. One important step in preventing angry outbursts is to recognize the sparks which ignite our personal flame of anger. Take a moment to ponder and reflect on the elements which usually lead to your personal outbursts. Think of the last time that you got angry with your family. Do you see a pattern of underlying frustrations which cause you to go over the edge (emotionally speaking)? Write these sparks on the lines below. As you look at them, examine why they make you angry. Perhaps you are a perfectionist, or you are trying to do things just like your mom. Maybe it is a pride issue or could it be rooted in a selfish desire.

Pray through possible solutions. Do you need to relax a little more when it comes to certain issues? Do you need to deal with past bitterness or current pride? Ask for God's help in recognizing and overcoming these areas.

Sparks which ignite my anger:

Why?

Solutions:

2. What Sends You?

As you write these thoughts, you are taking the first steps towards defeating potential angry outbursts. Reflect on these personal points as a reminder that we sometimes get agitated over things which are simply a reflection of our own personal pet peeves. Certainly, it is not worth demeaning those around us because our hot button was pushed. Disarm the hot button and begin the healing.

Personal Notes:

_____

_____

_____

_____

_____

_____

_____

_____

_____

_____

_____

_____

3. Music to Soothe the Soul

Music is a mood motivator. Our momentum and emotions can be effected by the style and rhythm of the music which surrounds us. Enhance a calm atmosphere in your home, by introducing peaceful, quiet instrumentals. Many studies have shown the positive effects of music on individuals, recognizing that calming music can induce a more relaxed state. Music therapy is based on the idea that music effects real change in our body's physiological make up in areas such as heart rate, breathing, blood pressure and even hormone levels.

The effect of music on the human spirit is not a new concept. In the Bible, we read about King Saul who had a "distressing spirit" (have you ever had one of those?) which troubled him. Saul's advisors told him to find a skillful player of the harp to calm his spirit. The lovely harp music played by David was Saul's sole relief (I Kings 16:14-23). What could the right music do for your home? It is worth exploring the possibilities. Your entire family may benefit from a visit to the music store. It is helpful to shop at a store which offers a "listening bar" or opportunities to preview (or pre listen) to the CDs before you purchase. A few types of music to consider are: Classical, Relaxation, Harp or Acoustic Guitar, Gentle Praise Music, Celtic Music. Experiment with the different rhythms and melodies to find music which calms your spirit. Some experts suggest music with a tempo slightly slower than your heart rate to offer true relaxation. You may enjoy playing music throughout the day or only a certain times. Choose the moments that best suit you and savor the soothing melodies as you surround your family with serenity.

3. Music to Soothe the Soul

Personal Notes:

_____

_____

_____

_____

_____

_____

_____

_____

_____

_____

_____

_____

_____

_____

_____

_____

_____

_____

_____

_____

_____

4. Activity Overload

Aaah - the land of opportunity! Isn't it wonderful to have millions of possibilities available for your precious young ones? From junior golf, to cheerleading, T-ball, ballet, basketball, gymnastics, piano, volleyball, tennis, swimming, art classes and more - many parents are running their kids and themselves ragged with activities. Parents do not want their children to miss an opportunity and therefore feel left out or have a bad self-image. Unfortunately, the overload of activities leads to stress and undo pressure in life as, families rush to practices, classes, tryouts and games. As parents, maybe it is time to step back and take a look at the big picture of life.

A good family goal is to raise kids of integrity and character, who use their gifts and talents to glorify God. The life goal should not be to create stressed out little six-year-olds, who participate in numerous activities and are not proficient at anything. As a general rule of thumb, when our children are young they should "dip their toes" into several activities to test the waters and see if they have an interest or talent in the area. As kids get older, it is time to narrow the field to their special interests, remembering they have schoolwork to accomplish as well. Parents should confer with their children, examining amount of practice time and games, and carefully, prayerfully decide which activities should be a part of their lives. Picture a pyramid, as your children build a base of many experiences when they are young and narrow down to the important as they grow older.

Adults must constantly reexamine their commitments as well.

(continued next page) 15

4. Activity Overload

It is easy to over-volunteer and serve in groups and committees thinking you are doing it for the betterment of the community. Are you enriching your families life by your over involvement? Keep the family as your first priority. Each year it is a good idea to reassess your schedule and weed out the excess, unfruitful activities from your calendar. Remember what your mother used to tell you when you went to a cafeteria? "Your eyes are bigger than your stomach, so don't put more on your tray than you are able to eat." We must be similarly guarded about the activities we put on our family plate. Prayerfully seek the best, not the busiest lifestyle for your family.

Personal Notes:

_____

_____

_____

_____

_____

_____

_____

_____

_____

5. Harmony with Hormones

Generally speaking, there are days when the kids spill the lemonade or walk on the carpet with dirty shoes, and you are able to emotionally handle it with a similitude of self-control. Then there are those days. The days when your husband just looks at you the wrong way, and you let loose like an exploding bomb, granting your spouse a fifteen minute lecture on being thoughtful and sensitive. How is it that women can be kind, nurturing and patient one day, and an angry, hotheaded witch on other days? It's called hormones and in order to have harmony with your hormones, you must have an understanding of them.

In her book *Women and Stress* (Revell, 99), Jean Lush describes the seasons that a woman's body goes through during each monthly cycle. The Spring phase represents the time during our menstrual cycle associated with the flow of blood and dominated by estrogen. Generally, a woman feels bright and positive during this time. The next phase described as Summer is a happy, creative time in which a woman feels pleased with life. Ovulation occurs during the summer phase. After ovulation comes Fall. During this phase, a woman begins to slowly lose energy while the doldrums or even slight depression sets in. Her husband and children do not seem quite as lovable during this part of the cycle. Confidence is droopy. Then Winter arrives around the fourth week of the cycle. Have you ever heard of the Snow Queen or Winter Witch? This would be her time to come out with numerous symptoms ranging from irritability (to say the least), mood swings and temper outbursts. In addition, she is less energetic, frustrated and easily rattled.

5. Harmony with Hormones

The good news is the menstrual flow is only a few days away and she will feel quite different then.

It is important for you to recognize these stages and acknowledge when you going through them. You may want to be extra careful not to overload your day or add undo stress during the Fall and Winter stages. It is also helpful to alert those around you that you are a little edgy during this time. Consider a small sign, flag, or banner to display for your family during your tense Winter moments. Perhaps it could say: "Don't Mess with Momma today." Or. "Careful, you are dealing with a Time Bomb." Whatever you do, do not use hormones as an excuse for unkind or out-of-control behavior. Simply use the hormone information to help you recognize your limits in order to adjust and work with your hormones.

Personal Notes: _____

_____

_____

_____

_____

_____

_____

_____

6. Rested Kids, Happy Mom

Amazing what a good night's sleep can do for the weary soul. As you well know from the midnight feedings time period in your home, you function better when you are well rested. Kids are no different. As they acquire sufficient amounts of sleep for their age, they function in a happier and well-adjusted manner. Give me a tired child, and I will give you a temper tantrum waiting to happen. You can prevent many potential meltdowns for both yourself and your children if you concentrate on making sure your child's sleep needs are met.

Here is a basic list of information for children's sleep requirements at different ages:

Newborn: A newborn baby will sleep whenever he needs to.

First Six Months: Leave daytime sleeping to him, naps will get shorter as he gets older

Six months to 1 year: 9 - 18 hours per day depending on the child. Usually 10 - 12 at night, plus 2 naps

1 year - 2 1|2 years: 13 hours plus one nap

Preschool years: 12 hours per day including nap

Elementary school years: 8 - 10 hours

Adolescents: 7 - 8 hours

source: Boston Children's Hospital Child Health Encyclopedia (Dell)

Keep in mind certain children vary in their need for sleep. Study your child and learn what his or her resting requirements are. A nap is a good idea for both mother and child during the early years. Keep the naptime as a regular routine until the school years. A summer schedule with a nap is highly suggested for any age. When your child outgrows "nap-time", rename the rest time with a title that sounds a little more grown-up. R & R (reading and relaxation), FOB (flat on back), Bunk time, Quiet time. A name is everything!

6. Rested Kids, Happy Mom

You are setting yourself up for screams if you toy with a tired toddler. For your own sanity as well as your kids, if at all possible, do not take a tired child to a restaurant, on errands or grocery shopping. During the younger years, it is helpful to keep a regular routine of rest for your child, running errands in between. Don't forget that your own rest is just as important. Make sure you are sleeping heartily and well at night. If you are restless at night, watch what you eat in the evenings and consider helpful products such as Melatonin. Remember, a hearty sleep can be the catalyst to a happy, energetic you!

Personal Notes:

_____

_____

_____

_____

_____

_____

_____

_____

_____

_____

Prescriptions for PEACE

7. Killing Klutter

"A place for everything and everything in its place." A good motto by which to live, yet a difficult one to keep in the day to day trenches of home life. Research documents the fact that people tend to remain in a calmer emotional state in surroundings that have less clutter. Everyone benefits from a well-organized environment, as it is easier to find needed items and important papers. God makes certain people naturally neat with all of their ducks in a row, while others are organizationally impaired and could use a little help. Here are a few tips to help the handicapped kill the clutter.

a) Take one room at a time - A big pill is hard to swallow. Break your clean up down to manageable sizes, and you will mentally be able to tackle your whole house before you know it. Choose one room per month that you will gradually reorganize. Write it on the calendar to keep it foremost on your mind. It is amazing what you can do by simply devoting 10 minutes a day to cleaning out a cupboard or shelf. Do it while you are on the phone or while the kids are sleeping.

b) Enlist the Help of an Organized Friend - Believe it or not, there are some people who love to help others organize a closet or room. When you discover a friend with this sort of interest; invite them over for lunch and a day of "fun" while you restore a room together.

c) Killer Saturdays - Designate every Saturday as the day you will go around the house and kill all the piles which have collected during the week (mail, "to do" piles, laundry, etc.).

7. Killing Klutter

d) The Right Stuff - Organization is much easier when you have the right bins and containers for storage. Make a list of your needs and visit the Dollar store or discount mart. Get items which are appealing to you so you will be motivated to use them.

e) Teach Them While They are Young - Help your kids learn the blessings of de-cluttering, by working with them to help organize their room. Then show them how to stay organized and pick up after themselves. Kids need a little initial help and time from you, but once you get the ball rolling, they will hopefully manage their own clutter.

Personal Notes:
_____
_____
_____
_____
_____
_____
_____
_____
_____

8. Planning Ahead for Possibilities

You can save yourselves much grief, heartache and screams by simply making use of wise planning. A doctor's office visit, a plane ride or a long wait at a restaurant can be a smooth sail if you bring the appropriate pacifiers. By pacifiers I not only mean baby's little binky. I'm referring to items which will meet physical needs, as well as dissuading boredom should the inevitable "long wait" occur. Here is a list of items to help you be prepared at all times.

a) Go-Go Bag - Many tantrums and challenging moments arise simply because the precious young ones are bored and need something which will keep their attention. Prepare a Go-Go bag for just such occasions. You want the items in your Go-Go bag to be special, fresh, and age-appropriate for your kids in order to hold their interest during those waiting moments. Consider items such as crayons (or markers), colored paper, new books, travel games and snacks.

b) Extra diapers and Change of Clothes - For young ones it is always possible an outfit will be "messed up" to the point of unwearability. Keep a change of clothing in the diaper bag or car for such a time as this.

c) Be Ready With a Bottle - Thank goodness for dry formula. Keep a bottle with a packet of dry formula, ready to make if your errand takes longer than you thought or your child suddenly is hungry again while you are waiting for your food at the restaurant.

d) Special Medicines - Always anticipate the possibility of your child's physical needs, especially if they are on special medication. I finally learned after several years of sniffles and sneezes to bring my daughters allergy medicine on every little excursion, just in case there was an unexpected cat or ragweed lurking.

8. Planning Ahead for Possibilities

Personal Notes:

_____

_____

_____

_____

_____

_____

_____

_____

_____

_____

_____

_____

_____

_____

_____

_____

_____

_____

_____

9. Mom's Diner

"You are what you eat," as the saying goes. Truly, the food you eat has an effect on your emotional state and your actions. As the food monitor for your families it is important to pay close attention to the nourishment needs for our kids. It is important for you to recognize the consequences of overloading you and your kids on certain foods. Always be aware and cautious of potential food allergies in your child. Here are several suggestions for nutritious and calming foods to load your shelves:

> Fruits and vegetables
> Nuts and seeds
> Yogurt, cheese and milk
> Meat, poultry and fish
> Beans, lentil, peas
> Whole grain breads and cereals

Best to Avoid:

> Sugar
> Caffeine
> High carbohydrates, non nutritious snacks
> Foods with preservatives
> Foods which cause allergic reactions (physical or behavioral)

Keep healthy snacks on your shelves such as trail mix, dried fruits and nuts. Begin to siphon out the snacks which are loaded in sugars and processed foods. Limit the amount of sodas and candy your children are allowed to eat each week. In our family, we have one "candy day" per week in which my kids may enjoy sugar-filled snacks. A wonderful resource for recipes and nutritional ideas for your family is Vicki Lansky's book *Feed Me I'm Yours*. 25

9. Mom's Diner

Mom's nutritious diner is essential to happy mom and happy kids. When people are hungry, they become cranky. Feed your children three healthy meals a day including nutritious snacks (mid-morning and|or mid-afternoon). An angry mood or fussy attitude many times can be attributed to a drop in blood sugar level in a person. Write a prescription for peace in your home by educating yourself in proper nutrition and becoming more aware of your family's needs.

Personal Notes:

_____

_____

_____

_____

_____

_____

_____

_____

_____

_____

_____

10. Exercise- You're Right!

Feel like a time bomb ready to explode? A brisk walk may be all you need to take the edge off and disarm the explosive. Studies show that exercise can boost energy, reduce anxiety and in some cases head off or banish depression. Why? Exercise releases neurochemicals called endorphins which are the bodies "natural relaxers." Exercise also distracts the mind and gives the brain a rest. As you concentrate on your physical activity, you can let your mind relax and forget about your cares for a short while.

A regular fitness program will not only help you look better, it will give you the lift that you need to make it through the day with energy and strength. As mothers, it may be difficult to find the time or opportunity to exercise. Here are some ideas to help.

a) The stroller is your friend- Bring the kids along as you exercise in the neighborhood. You get extra aerobic points for a double or triple stroller!

b) Exercise Pal- It helps to have a fitness partner to hold you accountable and help you stay on your routine. Plan to meet a friend early for an early morning walk while hubby is still at home to watch the kids or meet with strollers during the day.

c) Fitness center with Child care- Fitness establishments are finally catering to the multitude of potential "mommy customers" as many now provide tremendous day care while you work out. Check the ones in your area and enjoy your exercise while your kids have fun too!

10. Exercise- You're Right!

d) At Home- You have several options inside your own home. A workout video can be a good exercise program (your kids may even enjoy stretching along with you). If you have stairs in your home, you can create your own vigorous workout without a stair master. Leg weights can also be helpful as you strengthen your muscles with leg lifts while your kids watch the tube.

Find a program which you enjoy and works for you. Variety is the spice of life so vary the program now and then to stimulate your interest. Begin working out twice a week and progress eventually to three to five times per week, depending on your opportunities and schedule. You will see the benefits in your life both physically and emotionally as you feel stronger about yourself.

Personal Notes: _____

_____

_____

_____

_____

_____

_____

_____

_____

11. Lifelines

Mothers wear many hats. Child care director, chef, nurse, playground monitor, volunteer, loving wife, chauffeur, laundry lady, tutor, and the list goes on. It seems as though there is little time for anything other than managing the family, but mothers need a lifeline to the outside world. A devoted friend is a priceless gem in a woman's life. It takes time and care to nurture and develop a bonded friendship, yet the effort is worth the blessing. It is important to maintain friendships in order to have a co-heart with whom to share triumphs as well as troubles. An accountability mate, who shares your beliefs and faith will often encourage you in the right direction.

Do you have such a friend? Continue to devote yourself to the relationship, building a deeper bond and sharing these memorable child-rearing years of life together. Are you still searching for that kindred spirit? Be patient, but be proactive in looking for such a friendship. How do you develop a relationship with a friend when you are juggling so many other hats? A deep friendship can be a natural growth out of the acquaintances you know from your church, community, or other organizations. Within this pool of acquaintances keep a watchful eye for other ladies with whom you make a connection or have something in common. Plan a playgroup or a morning meeting at the park. Slowly build on the relationships which are already in your life and you will find that certain friendships will grow. Just as you can not force flowers to grow, you can not force the growth of a friendship, but with time and nurturing a friendship will develop.

11. Lifelines

As you deepen your soul-mate friendship, you will find you are making strides towards prescribing peace in your home. A friend is that cushion you can call when you are feeling overwhelmed. Sometimes a listening ear is just what the doctor ordered to make it though a frazzled day. Solomon said, "As iron sharpens iron, so one man sharpens another." Stay sharp, keep in touch, nurture your relationships.

Personal Notes:

_____

_____

_____

_____

_____

_____

_____

_____

_____

_____

Prescriptions for PEACE

12. Pictures of Perfection

Martha Stewart, I am not. The problem comes when I see all
that Martha creates, (along with her staff of 40 people) I tend to
think I should be doing similar presentations for my family and
friends. What picture of perfection do you hold in your mind?
May I encourage you to take the picture off the wall of your mind
and place it completely out of your view. Put in its place a realistic picture of a woman in charge of many responsibilities, the
most important being the training and nurturing or her
children. It is good to learn from others, but you must guard
against comparing yourself with others and creating unrealistic
expectations.

A perfectionist mode tends to create a frazzled woman. Why?
Because life is unpredictable, especially with children. Yes, your
precious little charges are human, and with any human being
comes the inevitable spills, mistakes, lagging behind and scattered
belongings. As peaceful women, you must be willing to let
certain things go, and learn to "not sweat the small stuff." This is
an easy task for certain people who are not easily rattled by little
messes or being a few minutes late. Other women live in anger
and frustration, because they can't seem to let the dirty dishes
slide for a few hours. Of course as with anything in life, there is a
balance. We can not become undisciplined slobs; on the other
hand, there are areas you can ease up on your grip.

Take a moment now to examine and reflect on areas in your life
which may have a perfectionist stronghold. As you write them
on the lines below, discover a healthy and realistic balance.
Ponder if it is really important to the well being of your family.
Look for ways you can still maintain discipline without the
frustrations, and remember always keep an eternal perspective!

12. Pictures of Perfection

Areas In Which I Have a Perfectionist Grip:

_____

_____

_____

_____

Healthy Balance:

_____

_____

_____

_____

Personal Notes:

_____

_____

_____

_____

_____

_____

_____

Keeping Your COOL
in the Heat of the Moment

Keeping Your COOL

Keeping Your COOL

1. STOP!
Learning to Gain Control

It's been an incredibly frustrating day filled with laundry, errands, playground duty and mud mess. Now to top it off, you shuffle the kids into the car one more time to zip to the post office in order to mail grandpa's late birthday gift and ---- they are closed! By this time, the kids are fighting in the back seat and you have no idea what you are going to serve for dinner. You feel like you are ready to scream at someone, and the kids are the most available victims. This is when you need to S.T.O.P! The letters in STOP each stand for a simple strategy to help you calm yourself and rethink the situation.

S - Step away. Physically take a few steps away from the kids. If possible step around a corner to remove yourself from the situation for a moment. (It goes without saying, if you are in a public place - do not leave your kids alone.)

T - Take a deep breath. Breath in slowly, hold your breath for a few seconds, exhale and relax. Repeat this several times.

O - Objectively examine the situation. Is this really important in the overall training of my children or is my anger out of control? Always remember that your children will learn the best lessons from your example. If you scream an instruction, what will they learn? If there is truly something they must learn from you, teach them calmly and it will be heard.

P - Pray for help from God to make it through the tense moments. Ask for His strength and emotional stability. See the prayer/poem in Section Four. It also helps to say a word of thanks to Him for your family naming each one by name.

1. STOP!
Learning to Gain Control

Use this easy acrostic as a formula to help you through the difficult times. Do not be discouraged or disappointed with yourself because of the feelings of rage you may feel due to challenges and aggravations. Life circumstances often bring major frustrations. Your feelings are not the enemy, what you do with them is. Remember the apostle Paul's words of wisdom, "In your anger, do not sin" (Ephesians 4:26). Recognize the feelings of rage rumbling like a volcano, and put a STOP to them before they overflow.

Personal Notes:

_____

_____

_____

_____

_____

_____

_____

_____

_____

_____

2. The Wonder of a Whisper

Savvy schoolteachers know the secret. Shouting gets you nowhere. If you want to have in impact on your audience, whisper the most important points. For some funny reason, people tend think a shout gets the point across in a dramatic way. Unfortunately, the increase in decibel level actually diminishes the effect of the message. Kids may hear you shouting, but they may not grasp what you are saying. If you want to make an impact with an important instruction, lower your voice to a whisper. As the kids strain to hear what you are saying, they will hear what you are saying.

A whisper takes the fear out of the message to your children and calms your spirit as well. As with any creative tool, overuse can cause it to lose its effectiveness. Choose wisely the pertinent points to say softly. Whether you choose to whisper or not, remember shouting or screaming is not the answer to the situation. I chuckle to think of the time or two I have shouted at my kids telling them to, "STOP YELLING AT EACH OTHER!!!" Certainly, a gentle response would be much more effective.

An interesting story in the Bible reminds us that God puts a value on whispering. You will find the fascinating story in I Kings 19:9 - 13 concerning Elijah. At a time in his life when he felt discouraged, disappointed and alone, Elijah received a message from God. The Lord told Elijah to stand on the mountain. A great and strong wind tore into the mountains, but the Lord was not in the wind. An earthquake came, but the Lord was not in the earthquake, then a fire, but the Lord was not in the fire. After the fire,

(continued next page)

2. The Wonder of a Whisper

there was a still small, whispering voice. Although God has great and mighty powers, He chose to speak to Elijah in a gentle whisper. Do you think Elijah got the message? In the same light, your kids will be blessed by your gentle and quiet spirit which is so pleasing in the sight of God (I Peter 3:4).

Personal Notes: _____

_____

_____

_____

_____

_____

_____

_____

_____

_____

_____

_____

3. Quick to Hear

You are probably familiar with the phrase, "Fools rush in, where angels fear to tread." This phrase offers an important lesson in life. Given a tense or volatile situation, the wise person waits to consider the circumstances, while fools rush in with little knowledge of the facts. Case in point, you hear the kids yelling at each other in the playroom upstairs. You can't quite make out the conversation, but you know it is not pretty. You have "had it up to here" with arguing and sibling unrest, and now you are ready to pounce like a hungry tiger on her prey. You crawl over the pile of laundry you are currently attempting to fold, dodge the toys on the stairs, fling open the door and scream, "Both of you to your rooms this instance."

"But mom."

"No, 'But mom to me.' I am sick and tired of hearing you fight with each other. Go to your rooms, and no snacks after nap time today!"

As they begin snivel and slink their way into their rooms, you hear a little voice, "But we were only pretending to be on a game show and shouting our answers."

OOPS! How many apologies could mommy avoid if she simply kept her composure and listened to the details before rushing in. Put a high priority on listening to your children. Perhaps a calm, listening mom is all a child needs to help him through a tantrum or frustration. An attentive ear can pick up on a need before it festers into a cry. In the book of James in the Bible we find just the advice we need, "Let every man (or mommy) be quick to hear, slow to speak and slow to wrath." Memorize these words as you become a more effective mother by using your two ears more than your one mouth.

3. Quick to Hear

Personal Notes:

_____

_____

_____

_____

_____

_____

_____

_____

_____

_____

_____

_____

_____

_____

_____

_____

_____

_____

_____

_____

_____

_____

4. Offering Thanks

You may not feel it at times, but you are thankful for your precious children as gifts from God, I'm certain. How often do you take the time to thank the Lord for the children He has given you? Take a moment right now to write down qualities and characteristics about your children for which you are truly thankful. Add to the list, areas that you do not enjoy. We need to thank God for the good and the bad, recognizing that both have their purpose. Offer thanks to God for the attributes in each of your kids. Do it right now.

Child's Name: Qualities and attributes for which I am thankful:

_____

_____

_____

_____

_____

_____

"..in everything give thanks for this is the will of God in Christ Jesus for you." I Thessalonians 5:18

There now, didn't that feel good? How did it make you feel toward your children? Keep this list in a convenient place. When you feel like shouting or pulling your hair out, just pull out this list instead and offer thanks for the gift of your children. It will do you good!

41

4. Offering Thanks

Personal Notes:

_____

_____

_____

_____

_____

_____

_____

_____

_____

_____

_____

_____

_____

_____

_____

_____

_____

_____

_____

5. A Stroll in the Park

Ahhh! A breath of fresh air. Yes, fresh air can do wonders for you in reducing pressure when you feel stressed or anxious. If you find you need a little calm therapy, step outside and take a brisk walk around the house or put the kids in the stroller and walk around the neighborhood for a few minutes. A park nearby may offer just the solace you need to find refreshment for your spirit. If you are working on a project and need to stay in the house, consider opening a window and feel the gentle fresh breeze on your face.

Have you ever noticed how peaceful you feel at the beach or in the country or other wide-open places. Space and fresh air counterbalance stress and anxiety. A stroll in the great outdoors can also be a quiet solace to relax your mind. Discover a place which is free from heavy traffic and construction noises. A quick walk, even around the backyard while the kids are inside can assist you through tense moments and potential outbursts. Take a jaunt outside in the late afternoon to take the edge off the typical pre-dinner stress.

Sunshine is another benefit to a walk in the park. Sunlight suppresses melatonin (the hormone which encourages sleep) and can actually help you stay more alert when late afternoon doldrums set in. Many times a slight boost of energy can help us make it through the rest of the day with a smile on our faces. If you need to take the kids, the walk will do them good as well, giving them a distraction from the normal routine.

5. A Stroll in the Park

Personal Notes:

_____

_____

_____

_____

_____

_____

_____

_____

_____

_____

_____

_____

_____

_____

_____

_____

_____

_____

_____

_____

6. Solitude in Silence

As you learned in Section One, music is a wonderful way to create a peaceful environment, but there are times when you may need a healthy dose of silence. Peace and quiet can sometime be just the right medicine to relax you and help you to unwind. A room void of game noises, washing machine sounds and television chatter can be pure joy. If you feel overwhelmed with life's responsibilities, worries, cares, and noises, then immerse yourself in soothing silence. In Psalm 4:4 we read David's words, "In your anger do not sin; when you are on your beds, search your hearts and be silent."

Often we fool ourselves into believing that we need noise to meet our emotional needs, just as some people use food to meet their emotional needs. Noise is not the solution. Television can actually be a stresser in your home. Keep it off as much as possible, contributing to the quietness in your abode. You will be amazed at the serenity you enjoy when you are not constantly being bombarded with voices, situations and advertisements. Many times when we need to think through a plan or a project or even tomorrow's schedule, we can think with a clear head if we can work in silence.

Is it practical or even possible to attempt to have peace and quiet with a house full of kids? Check out the quiet games listed in Section Three to help you with some silent kid activities. Depending on your children's ages and level of understanding, instruct your children to pretend to turn off their vocal chords (act as though there is an imaginary switch on their necks). Tell them to lay down on the carpet, close their eyes and listen to the quiet. Set a timer and tell the children when the timer goes off they may switch on their soft voices. Another way to achieve the elusive silence is to ask the kids to play quietly in their room while you enjoy solitude at the other end of the house. Naptime is another wonderful time for peace. Soak up silence and surround yourself with serenity.

6. Solitude in Silence

Personal Notes:

_____

_____

_____

_____

_____

_____

_____

_____

_____

_____

_____

_____

_____

_____

_____

_____

_____

_____

_____

_____

7. Sing It Out

Okay, okay, I know you just read instructions on the blessings of silent solitude, but pragmatically speaking there is a time and a place for singing in our lives as well. What better time than when we are about to explode. Picture yourself caught in rush hour traffic with a car full of hungry kids. You feel your tension level rising, what can you do? Turn on the radio or push in a tape and start singing! Encourage the kids to join in and you'll have a car full of choir kids singing their cares away. It worked for Julie Andrews and it can work for you.

What are some of your favorite tunes? Don't worry. You do not need to be a Celine Dion in order to belt out a melody with your kids. There are times when tired kids needs a terrific tune to lift their spirits, and it will give you a lift too. The kids will not judge you if you are incredibly off key (actually they probably will be too).

Purchase several sing along tapes to help you out. Here are some suggestions:

VeggieTunes from the VeggieTales series (Bob and Larry Publishing)

Wee Sing series (Price, Stern, Sloan) Bible Songs, Around the World, Nursery Rhymes, Fun and Folk

Children's Favorite Gospel Songs (Persnickety Press)

Winnie the Pooh, My First Sing Along Series

Your family may also enjoy movie soundtracks from a variety of their favorite movies.

47

7. Sing It Out

Personal Notes:

_____

_____

_____

_____

_____

_____

_____

_____

_____

_____

_____

_____

_____

_____

_____

_____

_____

_____

_____

8. Laugh It Off

Beth, a mother of four wonderful kids, remembers with a smile when her youngest son Kyle (age 4) decided to explore his artistic talent with tempera paint. No paintbrush or easel needed for this guy. Kyle decided it was much more creative to walk through the house with the paint bottles upside down, decorating the family room carpet and kitchen floor before he was abruptly stopped in the dining room. Beth had a choice. She could have completely lost it, or she could see the humor in the situation and realize this is a memory keeper. Thankfully, she chose the latter. After a good hearty laugh with the whole family and taking pictures of Kyle and his unique artistic creation, she then enlisted everyone's help in cleaning up the mess (especially the older child who left the paint out in the first place). They all had a good laugh and to this day they remember it as a humorous experience in their family's life. Can you imagine the memory made if Beth had chosen to scream? This is a true story, by the way!

There are those times when we need to see the humor in the situation. Laughter is the easiest available remedy for the distressed soul. Research has shown that laughter even increases the immune-system activity and tends to decrease stress hormones. Naomi Judd refers to laughter as "life's shock absorber," adding "laughter is to the soul what soap is to the body." (*Naomi's Home Companion*, GT publishing, 1997).

A hearty chuckle is a choice. Don't wait for the feeling, choose to take this frazzled moment and make it into a fun memory. There are numerous, humorous books available written by women looking at the funnier side of life. I keep one in my car at all times

49

8. Laugh It Off

in case I need a lift while I am waiting in carpool line or at the doctor's office. So next time you walk into the kitchen and the pot roast is missing, but a bloated dog is lying under the table, take a moment to laugh and make joyful memories in the process. Then drive through Burgers-R-Us for dinner!

Personal Notes:

_____

_____

_____

_____

_____

_____

_____

_____

_____

_____

_____

_____

_____

_____

9. Five-Minute Retreats

A blissful stroll down a deserted beach. A mountain hideaway with only you and a good book. Solitude can be a good thing. Unfortunately, the job description of a mother does not include lengthy periods of "alone time." Although vacations can be carefully planned and baby-sitters dutifully employed, there are still those times in the heat of the day when mom needs instant relief from the people surrounding her. Since she can't catch the next plane to Bermuda, a five-minute retreat may be just what mom needs to make it through the rest of the day.

The question surfaces, where do you go for such a retreat? Here are some retreat spaces suggested by fellow frazzled moms:

a) Bathroom - Locks on door, facilities available, plus a place to sit.

b) Master bedroom - Usually has a lock on door, bed to lay down.

c) Large walk-in closet - Quiet, private and hard for little ones to locate mom.

d) Laundry room - Not a dream vacation, but if it is big and has room for a chair, it can work.

Perhaps you are wondering how you step out of the situation when the precious dumplings are getting on your nerves and you feel you are at wits end. There are several creative ways. Again here are ideas from fellow "sisters in search of solitude."

Tell the kids you need to step into the other room for just a moment. Give strict instructions, you are not to be disturbed for five minutes (set a timer). As you may already know, young ones do not always understand these instructions, so the locked door may come in handy.

9. Five-Minute Retreats

Put a 5-minute retreat sign or surrender flag in full view of everyone. Explain what the sign means, and help your family understand your need to step away sometimes.

What do you do during your retreat from the natives? Calm down, take several deep breaths, close your eyes, pray, regroup, look over your list of kid qualities for which you are thankful, read or rest. Caution: do not overuse or abuse the retreat idea. It should be a fairly rare occurrence. If you retreat too often, the kids will not respect the boundaries you have set and will not leave you alone. Use the 5-minute retreat as a desperate measure for desperate times when you truly need a few minutes to rejuvenate and remind yourself that you do love this job!

Personal Notes: _____

_____

_____

_____

_____

_____

_____

_____

_____

10. Apologize from the Heart

It happens to everyone. Yes, losing your temper is not uncommon to the human race. Moms are especially vulnerable to those frazzled, stressed-out moments that seem to get the better of us. Certainly we want to minimize these times for the sake of our children's gentle and moldable self-esteem. Although we are human, we must seek God's help to maintain a gentle spirit and self-control. When we occasionally "lose it" with the kids, we should not be overcome with guilt. It is important to recognize that we are not perfect, but continuing to grow to be more like Christ.

Upon the rare occasion that you do lose your temper or scream at the kids, an apology is a vital part of the healing process. Your children will learn from your sincere and humble spirit, as well as your desire to set things right. Your example will also teach them how to apologize when it is their turn (and most likely it will be their turn soon). Your apology should not consist of idle words, but rather it should reflect a truly repentant heart. Never use an apology as an excuse to do the offense again. Hopefully, knowing that you will need to say you are sorry if you lose your temper should help you limit your anger, slow down and regroup.

Perhaps you are thinking, "But my child needs a strong scolding, so I shouldn't apologize to him." Actually, children never need screaming from an out-of-control adult. What disobedient children do need is training and disciple handled with temperance and love. Ephesians 4:29 reminds us, "Let no corrupt communication proceed out of our mouth, but what is good for necessary edification, that it may impart grace to the hearers." Saying you are sorry speaks volumes to your kids and reminds us all that we are human indeed.

10. Apologize from the Heart

Personal Notes:

Keeping Your COOL

11. Relaxing Exercises

Not able to visit the spa on a regular basis? You can actually do a few things at home which may make you feel you have had a short excursion away. Try these tension relievers:

a) Stress-squeeze Ball - You can purchase squeeze balls from most novelty shops or health stores. Make your own using a water balloon. Cut the neck off of the top of the balloon and fill the balloon with corn starch or flour. Cut the top and bottom off another balloon and fit it over the ball you just made, covering the opening. Add a few more cut balloons until it is secure from leakage. Enjoy squeezing the stress away in the palm of your hand.

b) Neck Relaxer - Ease tension and tension headaches with this easy to make relaxation enhancer. You will need one long sock (should be no problem to find a sock waiting for its mate to show up) and two tennis balls. Place the tennis balls down in the sock and tie a knot at the top. Now lie on the floor with your feet propped up on a chair or couch. Rest your neck on your homemade relaxer with the center of your neck nestled between the two balls. Just lay there and let the balls pressing against your pressure points do the rest.

d) Soothing Sandals - A mother rarely has the opportunity to sit down, and this tends to take a toll on our feet. Foot discomfort can lead to aches in the legs and lower back, creating more stressful feelings during the day. One way to receive some foot therapy during a trying day is to purchase inexpensive massage sandals.

55

11. Relaxing Exercises

As you walk in these sandals, hundreds of little rubber spikes massage the bottom of your feet, giving you relief and comfort. Available at most athletic shoe stores; try some on for size and stress reduction!

e) A Ball For Your Feet -   Sit down and take off your shoes. This tension reliever deals with the feet, but actually helps relieve tension throughout most of the body as accesses many pressure points which are located in the feet. Place a tennis ball beneath the arch of your foot. Move the ball from toes to heel using a slight downward pressure back and forth. Try two minutes for each foot.

Personal Notes: _____

_____

_____

_____

_____

_____

_____

_____

_____

12. Life, Love and Hugs

Life has its moments; some which are gloriously wonderful, while other moments are deeply disappointing. What may seem insignificant to you as an adult, may appear gigantic to your child. Perhaps you do not understand why your child would cry over a small incident such as the wheel falling off his truck. To you, life is much bigger than a broken toy, but keep in mind, you have had years to mature and figure out this great life lesson. Your child is young. Instead of scolding him for having an eschewed picture of life, help him through it. Many cries and tantrums are simply life lessons waiting and wanting to be taught.

Consider how shepherds handle their sheep. They gently nudge and prod them and lead them to green pastures and still waters. As a shepherd to your little lambs, take a lesson from the Good Shepherd who did not scold his disciples when they did ridiculous things or asked stupid questions. He carefully, lovingly led them along to slowly understanding the big picture in life.

There are times for discipline, but there are also times for a loving hug of understanding. A hug can be the calming relief when a child is overly upset and needs a peaceful reassurance that it will be okay.

Be generous with loving kindness and hugs. There are times when a group hug is needed. When everyone is out of sorts, call for a group hug to disarm the frustration. It will do everyone a bit of good (including mom!). It is fun to have a signal which represents "time for a hug."

Putting both arms in the air can be the nonverbal cue to prepare for a loving embrace. Scripture tells us, "Love covers a multitude of sins." One hug speaks volumes as it speaks to your child, "it will be okay." Whether you feel over stressed or your child is having a breakdown, replace your frustration with a warm, gentle hug.

12. Life, Love and Hugs

Personal Notes:

_____

_____

_____

_____

_____

_____

_____

_____

_____

_____

_____

_____

_____

_____

_____

_____

_____

_____

_____

_____

QUIET
Activities for Kids

QUIET
Activities for Kids

1. Lay Down and Listen
2. Puzzle Pictures and Pick-Up Sticks
3. Mold it and Make it
4. Silent Story and Reading Cubby
5. Happy Hands
6. Fun with Flannel
7. Bed Tents at Camp Sheets
8. Roxy
9. Bunny Games
10. Computer Companion
11. Central Mailroom
12. S.O.S.- Saved Objects for
    Special Times

QUIET Activities for Kids

1. Lay Down and Listen

Here's a group game to help you relax and lighten your load. This resourceful game will slow down the kids and help them to enjoy the peaceful calm as well!

You will need: a variety of items which make subtle and unique sounds. Consider boxes with lids, spoons, sandpaper, comb, Velcro, cellophane, crackers, etc.

Ask kids to lie down on the carpet and close their eyes. Mom sits in the center of the room and tells the kids to listen carefully. Participants are to raise their hands when they hear a noise, but they are not to say a word. Start by letting the children listen to the natural noises around the house such as the dryer or refrigerator or a dog barking. After they have listened to several natural noises, then one by one mom uses the items she gathered to make a variety of noises. Space the noises at different intervals of time so the kids do not know when to expect them.

Change the rules later to let the kids talk, while still keeping their eyes shut. Allow them to describe the item they think they are hearing. See if they can guess correctly. Count how many sounds the kids heard from the natural noises around the house. This is a relaxing game which also helps your children to be more attentive to what they are hearing.

1. Lay Down and Listen

Personal Notes:

_____

_____

_____

_____

_____

_____

_____

_____

_____

_____

_____

_____

_____

_____

_____

_____

_____

_____

_____

2. Puzzle Pictures and Pick Up sticks

You will need:
    Magazine
    Glue sticks
    Scissors
    Poster board.

First, create a unique puzzle. Allow the kids to search through magazines to each find a beautiful picture which they enjoy or like. Try to find pictures which cover most of the page. Glue the picture onto poster board, trimming off the edges. After it is dry, cut (mom does this for the little ones) the puzzle into long strips about ? inches wide. Now your picture has become a puzzle.

Play Pick Up Sticks: Gather your puzzle strips in one hand and drop them on the table letting them gently fall into a pile. To make a challenge for older kids (9 and up) combine the pieces to each of the puzzles in one pile, while younger kids may want to keep each puzzle in a separate pile. Now play pick up sticks as one person at a time tries to pick up the strips without making any of the other pieces move. Each player continues their turn until they accidentally make another piece move. In that event, play goes to the next player. When all sticks are picked up, count to see who was able to get the most. With numerous kids or players, you may have several games taking place at once.

Put the Puzzle together: When the Pick Up Sticks game is over, have a contest to see who can put their puzzle together first.

2. Puzzle Pictures and Pick Up sticks

Personal Notes:

_____

_____

_____

_____

_____

_____

_____

_____

_____

_____

_____

_____

_____

_____

_____

_____

_____

_____

QUIET Activities for Kids

3. Mold it and Make it

Working with your hands, molding and making sculptures can be wonderful, quiet therapy for both kids and adults. Make this dough ahead of time if you like, so you will always have it on hand when in need of a quiet moment.

You will need:
2 cups flour
1 cup salt
4 Tbsp. Cream of tartar

2 cups water
2 Tbsp. oil
food coloring

Mix flour, salt and cream of tartar in a medium sized cooking pot. Stir in the wet ingredients including food coloring. Mix well. Stir over medium heat for three to five minutes or until the dough pulls away from the sides of the pan and forms a big ball. Place dough on surface covered with wax paper and lightly sprinkled with flour. Allow to cool.

Now the kids can have fun kneading the cooled dough until it gets nice and smooth. Your dough can be stored in plastic sealed bags or containers for later use. If it dries out, add a few drops of oil or water to it and knead until it is soft and smooth again.

Here are some suggestions for what the kids can make:
Snakes
Figures made using cookie cutters
Dinosaurs
Build castles using plastic tubs
Pottery
Make play food and serve a meal
Houses, forts, villages
Flowers

3. Mold it and Make it

Personal Notes:

_____

_____

_____

_____

_____

_____

_____

_____

_____

_____

_____

_____

_____

_____

_____

_____

_____

_____

_____

4. Silent Story and Reading Cubby

Yes, mommy loves to read stories to her precious little ones, but there are times when mommy needs a break from reading aloud. Here's a happy solution for wonderful bookworm quiet time.

You will need:
Tape recorder with headphones
Books with coordinating tape (or prerecorded mom reading on tape)
Several pillows
Special space for cubby

Plug your child into a good book as they listen with their headphones and snuggle up in a special place. Location is every-thing. A small little area can be transformed into a reading cubby by adding a few pillows. Areas to consider are a large closet, under the dining room table, large box, corner of a room boxed off with cushions. Let your imagination go wild!

Excellent books on tape for your consideration:

Share A Story series includes many great titles
    (Harper's Children's Audio)
Barney Story Hour (The Lyons Group)
Thomas the Tank and Friends (Random House)
Clifford series (Scholastic Books and Cassettes)
Curious George series (Houghton Mifflin)
Arthur series (Little, Brown and Company)
Madeline series (Puffin Story Tapes)

4. Silent Story and Reading Cubby

Personal Notes:

_____

_____

_____

_____

_____

_____

_____

_____

_____

_____

_____

_____

_____

_____

_____

_____

_____

_____

_____

5. Happy Hands

All hands on deck to help out around the house and have fun in the process. Perhaps you have heard the phrase, "Busy hands are happy hands," or "Many hands make light work." Give the hands in your home an opportunity to help mom and have fun in the process. The purpose of this project is to help mother with some of those looming chores which are difficult to accomplish while tending to little ones. Make this a quiet activity by encouraging the kids to work their hands not their mouths as we silently sweep away the chores. If you are in the mood for a little music, turn on an enjoyable melody which will inspire and motivate your workers.

In order to make an official "happy hands" introduction, purchase inexpensive work gloves at a discount store. Let your kids choose a colorful pair for themselves or purchase white work gloves and let the kids decorate them with markers. After chores, keep the gloves on a special shelf to be used the next time you play Happy Hands.

Now the little hands are ready for work. How can you make work fun? Start with your own attitude of excitement toward accomplishing something for the household. Motivate the kids by telling them about the snack they will be able to enjoy when they finish. Give specific instructions (explained in a positive way) as to what their job is and what areas they need to stay away from. Here are some Happy Hand suggestions for chores:

a) Inside/outside windows - While one person cleans the inside of a window or glass door, another person simultaneously cleans the outside of the glass. Tell them to follow each others hands and try to make a mirror image.

5. Happy Hands

b) Biggest Weed Contest - Tackle the weeds outside by getting everyone into the process.

c) Car Wash - Quite a blast when everyone works together.

d) Clutter Free Closet Contest - All participants examine the cluttered closet and write down a guess as to how long it will take to clean it out. Then everyone works against the clock to clean the closet. The person with the closest time guess wins a prize.

e) Garage Kids - Write down on separate pieces of paper every task which needs to be accomplished in order to get the garage spic and span. Put all the slips of paper in a basket and let everyone chose a chore. Then go to it!

f) Raking it in - Work as teams or individuals creating the biggest piles of leaves in the yard. Work together to bag the results. Give a prize to the person or team with the highest pile and the most bags.

Happy Hands has its rewards as everyone feels better when the task is accomplished. Remember to make the tasks age appropriate to prevent frustration. Enjoy the time of peace and work together as you work your worries away with your wonderful family.

Personal Notes:
_____
_____
_____
_____

6. Fun with Flannel

A flannel board can offer a wonderful time of quiet creativity as children decorate with scenes and stories. Once you have gathered the materials and made the initial flannel board, your kids will enjoy creating figures to be used on the board for stories and games.

You will need:

Lightweight plywood board or wall board (18" by 24")
Flannel material (22" by 28") (Use light blue for outdoor scenes and beige for indoor scenes)
Strong tape duct tape

To make the flannel board, simply pull the material tight around the board, securing it with tape in the back. Tape a second color only to the top in order to flip over to change indoor to outdoor scenes.

To create people and extras you will need:

Additional colors of flannel
Old Magazines, Greeting Cards and pictures
Scissors
Velcro((self adhesive)

If the kids are old enough to use the scissors (5 and up) allow them to cut out pictures of people and places to use on their flannel board. Attach a piece of the Velcro((rough hooked side) to the backs of pictures. Using other colorful pieces of flannel, kids can cut tree shapes, rocks and a long stretch of grass.

Kids can have hours of quiet fun as they develop a story or play to present to parents later in the day. They can tell a well-known story or make up their own. Kids can trade jobs as storyteller, person placer or prop person to make a memorable flannel production. Children may also want to play Tic Tac Toe by making the Xs and Os from index cards and placing Velcro on the back.

6. Fun with Flannel

Personal Notes:

_____

_____

_____

_____

_____

_____

_____

_____

_____

_____

_____

_____

_____

_____

_____

_____

_____

_____

7. Bed Tents at Camp Sheets

(Ages 3-9) For an afternoon of serene pleasure, send the kids off to camp. Camp Sheets that is! Their own bedroom can become a campy playland by making their bed into a tent. How do you make a bed tent? First pull back the heavy bed covers, spreads or blankets. Next set an object between the sheets to lift up the top sheet and provide air space in the tent. A child-safe umbrella (open) works well or you can even use the kids plastic furniture, such as little chairs or tables. Be careful and remember safety first when it comes to bed tent building (no folding chairs, etc).

Now encourage the kids to use their imagination as to the rest of the camp grounds in the bedroom. Stuffed animals can become animals to be tracked in the wild. A blanket on the floor can become a fishing pond complete with fish. Create fish by cutting a fish shape from construction paper and attaching a paper clip to one end. Give your child their own fishing pole. Make a pole with the cardboard tube from a hanger, string attached and magnet on the end. Harmonicas, compasses, maps and story books make the camping experience complete.

A bedroom is not limited only to a camping theme. Other possibilities for adventures include a rocket ship on the bed and bedroom becomes alien planet. Or consider the bed as a boat and the rest of the room is the ocean. Let the kids continue to imagine and create as you encourage them to enjoy creative play in their own rooms. Once you get them started, then close the door and allow the kids to have hours of subdued and quiet fun.

7. Bed Tents at Camp Sheets

Personal Notes:

_____

_____

_____

_____

_____

_____

_____

_____

_____

_____

_____

_____

_____

_____

_____

_____

_____

_____

8. Roxy

(Ages 4 - 15) Here's a new version of an old Native American game used with stones and symbols.

First you will need to collect 21 rocks or stones which can fit into the palm of your hand. You may enjoy going on a family walk, hike or rock hunt for the preparation of this game. If you have limited rock possibilities around your house, visit a local nursery which will most likely have some for sale. Using craft paints or nail polish, paint the following symbols on the rocks.

    7 rocks with circles on them

    7 rocks with x's on them

    7 rocks with the letter "z" symbol on them

    Allow plenty of time for the paint on the rocks to dry.

You will also need an old pillowcase. You may want to allow the kids to decorate the pillowcase, coloring pictures or symbols on it with markers.

How you play: Place the dried rocks in the pillowcase and mix them up. Each person then takes turns drawing out a rock which they set in a pile in front of them. When all the rocks are drawn, it is time to examine the piles. Each player will separate his or her rocks into X, O, and Z piles. The player who ends up with the most of one kind of stone is the winner. You can play as many rounds as you like to see who ends up being the overall winner. Record your scores on a pad or poster.

Rock, Tac, Toe: You can also play a version of tic, tac, toe using the rocks as your markers. Create a tic, tac, toe board on poster board or better yet on the side of the pillowcase. You can play over and over again using your X and O stones.

8. Roxy

Personal Notes:

_____

_____

_____

_____

_____

_____

_____

_____

_____

_____

_____

_____

_____

_____

_____

_____

_____

_____

QUIET Activities for Kids

9. Bunny Games

(Ages 2 - 5) Quiet as a bunny! Introduce this game by presenting bunny ears to each of the players. Bunny ears can be made by simply taking white typing paper and cutting long thin ovals for ears. Use pink crayon or marker to color the interior of the ear. Glue the ears to visors or headbands and you have instant bunnies. To help the kids further play the part, use face makeup for nose and whiskers. White socks on the hands is another added extra. Once you have created a house full of bunnies ask the kids what kind of noise a bunny makes. They may have to think about it for a moment but soon they will realize that bunnies for the most part are very quiet animals. Now it is time to play some bunny games with the quiet tone in mind.

a) Bunny Hop - Provide a hopping course for your bunnies. You can use throw pillows, carpet squares, place mats, fabric squares or masking tape to make a trail of squares on which the bunnies can jump. You may want to lead them on an obstacle course using boxes, chairs and tables for tunnels.

b) Carrot Hunt - Make some carrots out of construction paper or use a bag of baby carrots from the fridge to create a little scavenger hunt for your bunnies. Give them each baskets or bags to collect their carrots. After one round, let one of the bunnies hide the carrots for the next round.

c) Leap Bunny - Teach the bunnies how to play Leap Frog, bunny style.

d) Bunny Craft - Provide paper plates and construction paper and let your bunnies create a bunny face.

e) Bunny Video or Book - To cap off a "bunny day" read a story or watch a video with a bunny theme.

9. Bunny Games

Personal Notes:

_____

_____

_____

_____

_____

_____

_____

_____

_____

_____

_____

_____

_____

_____

_____

_____

_____

_____

10. Computer Companion

The computer is your friend. Kids need time to enjoy the computer just as much as you need a few quiet moments. Discover fantastic computer programs which cover a wide range of ages and teach a multitude of concepts and ideas. Take time to read the information about the program. Introduce the program to your children and teach them how to use it. As the kids get older, teach them how to access the different programs on your computer so they can go right to their favorites. Your initial investment to show them how it works, will pay off in pleasant learning times for your children. Many computer stores and children's learning stores offer help in finding just the right program for your family as well as simple instructions on how to use the program.

Check out some of these kid tested favorites:
Reader Rabbit series (The Learning Company)
Math Blaster series (Knowledge Adventure)
Great Adventures for ages 3-7 (Fisher Price)
Learning Center series (Davidson)
Jump Start Baby (Knowledge Adventure)
Millie and Bailey Preschool (Edmark)

Remember, the computer is not a baby-sitter. Do not overuse it and set limits on the time for each child. The computer should be a helpful companion in your home to allow your kids to have positive learning experiences.

10. Computer Companion

Personal Notes:

_____

_____

_____

_____

_____

_____

_____

_____

_____

_____

_____

_____

_____

_____

_____

_____

_____

_____

_____

11. Central Mailroom

(Ages 2 - 9) Create an entire mail system within your home, letting your kids deliver the mail. First you will need to create mailboxes for each person in your household.

You will need:

Shoe boxes

Construction or wrapping paper

Tape

Markers and stickers

Scissors

Cover the boxes with paper, taping the edges to secure the paper. Color and decorate the boxes with marker and stickers. Mom should cut a large flap on the top of each box to allow mail to go in and be retrieved. Put each family member's name on their box. Now place the boxes outside of their bedrooms either on a chair or on the floor.

The kids can then create mail. Using stationery, typing paper and envelopes allow them to decorate, write and create mail. Old magazines can make good mail. Also, some magazines have new subscription cards in them which can be used as post cards for the mail. It doesn't matter if the kids can write yet or not, as they can draw pictures or scribble letters. Use stickers or stamps for the stamp in the corner. Perhaps you have some old address labels for the return address on the envelopes.

Make mail carrier bags out of grocery sacks, cutting away the top half of the bag and using the cut off portion to fold as a strap. Once the postmen have gathered the mail, they must take it to the central mail room and sort it to the different recipients.

11. Central Mailroom

If you have an ink pad and rubber stamps, then let the kids stamp the mail before delivery. After a day of play, put away the post office paraphernalia for another day of quiet play in a few weeks.

Personal Notes:

_____

_____

_____

_____

_____

_____

_____

_____

_____

_____

_____

_____

_____

_____

_____

_____

12. S.O.S.-
Saved Objects for Special Times

(Ages 2 - 12) When mom's emotional ship of strength is sinking, it is time for S.O.S.

Saved Objects for Special times represent toys, games and activities which are kept hidden away, only to be brought out in the moment of need. Yes, "Absence makes the heart grow fonder" even between kids and toys. Save away a few specific games or toys which can be used without a tremendous amount of supervision or instruction. Special quiet activities which keep the kids interest when mom needs a rest. Here are some suggestions:

a) White Wipe off Board and Markers - Crayola© makes a fun, nylon zippered case which includes white board, markers, eraser and paper. A fun little self contained activity.

b) For Girls - Doll with accessories. Keep all the items in a plastic storage bin. Girls will enjoy playing with this doll as it only comes out at special times. This may be a fashion doll or a baby doll according to your daughter's interest. Paper or wooden dolls with change of clothes are also a great delight.

c) For Boys - A set of special cars or trucks stored in an air tight container can provide special times for boys. Add a fold out road system the kids have their own contained area in which to play. You can purchase road boards or make your own from a large square of felt.

d) Doctor's Kit - Another case full of quiet play for boys or girls.

e) Puzzle Party - If you child loves puzzles, purchase or make a few special sets to be stored away for S.O.S.

12. S.O.S.-
Saved Objects for Special Times

f) Quiet blocks - Soft blocks (cotton-covered foam) come in many shapes and sizes and offer special, quiet play for building forts or houses.

In preparing S.O.S. toys for your kids, recognize the individual tastes and interests of each child. You may choose to give them a game to play together, but this does open up the possibilities for sibling arguments. I believe it is best to give each child their own S.O.S. activity along with some personal space, so they will not be challenged by siblings. Keep your S.O.S. closet updated and age-appropriate. Older kid's toys can be passed down to the younger ones.

The key to S.O.S. is to bring out the objects only occasionally to build the desire and interest in playing with the items.

Personal Notes: _____

_____

_____

_____

_____

_____

_____

_____

MOMMY
Moments

MOMMY Moments

1. The Fellowship Factor

2. Marvelous Messages

3. Personal Pleasures

4. Relish a Good Book

5. Creative Outlet

6. Delightful Drinks

7. Life's Lesson Plans

8. Joy Journal

9. Nap Time for Mom

10. Soak Away Stress

11. Memory Lane

12. A Mother's Prayer

MOMMY Moments

1. The Fellowship Factor

Two are better than one, because they have a good reward for their labor. "For if they fall, one will lift up his companion." - Ecclesiastes 4:9,10

As much as some of us may pride ourselves in being "an island unto ourselves," we really do need each other. Fellowship with other women is a strengthening factor in one's life. We need good healthy positive relationships to encourage us down life's roads. There are many opportunities for mothers to find fellowship with other women and usually child care is provided. It may take a little effort, but it is an important refreshment in your life. As one mother of preschoolers put it, "I desperately need to talk with people above the age of six." Conversation with preschoolers does have its limitations. Look for opportunities in your community to relish the benefits of fellowship with mothers.

Start with a local church. If you are not involved in a church, begin finding one which shares your beliefs. Your family will be richly blessed by the connections you make in your community through church friendships. Your kids need the opportunity as well to grow up in a church environment, learning about God's word and making new friends. Most churches offer a mothers group, gathering or Bible study. Seek one out at your church and if there is not one, perhaps you could be the one to get it started!

Other national groups which have chapters in most communities include: MOPs (Mother's of Preschoolers), Early Childhood PTA, Moms Clubs, Preschool PTA. You may also want to explore nondenominational Bible studies such as BSF, Community Bible study or Precepts Ministries. Stay connected with other mothers and you will find yourself refreshed from factor of fellowship in your life.

1. The Fellowship Factor

Personal Notes:

_____

_____

_____

_____

_____

_____

_____

_____

_____

_____

_____

_____

_____

_____

_____

_____

_____

_____

_____

MOMMY Moments

2. Marvelous Massages

Massages are a time proven way to reduce the physical effects of your tensions and stress. A regularly scheduled massage would do wonders for most women. Unfortunately, it is impractical to suggest that busy mothers take time from the daily routine to indulge in an hour-long body massage. The good news is there are some practical ways a mother can access the benefits of a massage with in her lifestyle.

Relaxing Self Massage - Massage therapy is best when applied by another person, but there are a few techniques which you can do to soothe and relax yourself. Try these:

a) Head massage - much like a shampoo rub. Spread fingers and use slow firm pressure as you rub your scalp in a circular fashion.

b) Hand Massage - Give your hands a relaxing massage using one of your favorite, soothing lotions. Allow one hand to gently rub the other, beginning with your entire palm and then massaging each individual finger.

c) Gentle Face Massage - Using two fingers, gently rub in a circular motion a various areas on your forehead. Next, massage around your cheekbone, the sides of your nose, under your eyebrows and along your jawbone. You will discover certain areas feel relaxing to you, so repeat the massage in those areas.

d) Marriage Massage: Enhance your relationship with your spouse by giving each other back rubs or neck massages. Try to find a time when you are not rushed and both have time to relax without the kids. Perhaps a Saturday morning or evening night after the kids are in bed. Discuss with each other what you both like and need from a massage. You will both benefit from the refreshment and relaxation and possibly give a new glow to your marriage as well!

2. Marvelous Massages

d) Other Relaxing Ideas: Facials and chair massages can be an easy and special way to enjoy a treat for yourself. Look for specials or coupons or let your family know you wouldn't mind a gift certificate for a holiday or birthday. For specific tension areas in your body there are electronic neck and back massagers which are available at department stores and gadget stores. Electronic or hydraulic foot massages can give your feet a new lease on life as well. Keep in mind that our bodies tend to tense up when we are carrying anxiety and stress, so the best muscle relief of all is to give your anxieties to God each day.

Personal Notes:

_____

_____

_____

_____

_____

_____

_____

_____

_____

MOMMY Moments

3. Personal Pleasures

Time for a little self examination. What is it that you truly enjoy? Not what your husband enjoys, but what is it that relaxes you and makes you feel wonderful? Massages may be nice, but maybe a manicure makes your day. Perhaps it is a wonderful dessert at one of your favorite cafes. Could it be a Mocha Grande and a good book at the local bookstore? Write down a few pleasures which you personally find restoring and wonderful.

As a mother, you may not be able to indulge in a personal pleasure on a regular basis, but now and then attempt to scheduled some moments of pure joy into your life. These excursions should be short, inexpensive and fairly infrequent in order to remain special and easy to do. If necessary, hire a baby sitter for a short pleasure outing or ask a family member to help. Discuss your list with your husband. Ask him to make a list as well. Talk about ways you can help each other to fit enjoyable moments into your schedules.

You will find that scheduling a short opportunity to do something you enjoy will give you a lift and something to look forward to each month. It is a good idea to allow your family to know of some of the pleasures on your list in order for them to know potential gifts or gift certificates for future birthdays, Mother's day and Christmas. This relieves some of the mystery and frustration which may arise each year as to what to get mom.

3. Personal Pleasures

Personal Notes:

_____

_____

_____

_____

_____

_____

_____

_____

_____

_____

_____

_____

_____

_____

_____

_____

_____

_____

_____

_____

4. Relish a Good Book

Picture a beautiful pink Victorian home with a wide wooden porch. Imagine yourself sipping mint tea as you swing on the white hanging porch swing while chatting with your friends. A good book can take you away to a different time or place. Relishing a book, whether fiction or nonfiction offers a wonderful retreat for you in your own home and open up a new world to you. Consider a lovely "coffee table" book, with pictorial scenes and brief yet informative descriptions. A lovely art book viewing life from a talented artist's point of view. A book of poetry accompanied by lovely floral scenes. Even a cookbook can be a pleasure to thumb through picking up new ideas and recipes. Books such as these can be a splendid way to take a mini-vacation away from life's responsibilities for even a short while.

Mothers may not have the time to read a full text whether it is fiction or nonfiction. In fact, attempting to read a deep or involved book may become frustrating and lead to more tension than it is worth. Busy women may best tune into quick-read books.

Here are a few suggestions to read for refreshment:

Simplicity: Finding Peace by Uncluttering Your Life by Kim Thomas (Broadman & Holman)

Mother's Garden of Prayer by Sarah Maddox & Patti Webb (Broadman & Holman)

Take Time: A Moment for the Heart by Melody Carlson (Broadman & Holman)

Everyday Miracles: Unexpected Blessings in a Mother's Day by Dale Hanson Bourke (Broadman & Holman)

Mom, You're Incredible: Celebrating the Power of Motherhood by Linda Weber (Broadman & Holman)

4. Relish a Good Book

Other books to consider: poetry, cookbooks

A word of caution concerning fiction books. There are some women who can become addicted to fiction books to the detriment of those around them. Be careful not to let your love for reading get the best of you. Read novels which place a value on purity and morality and always be cautious about allowing fiction to make you disappointed with your own situation.

Personal Notes:

_____

_____

_____

_____

_____

_____

_____

_____

_____

_____

_____

MOMMY Moments

5. Creative Outlet

"Creativity has been built into every one of us; it's part of our design." Ted Engstrom

We each have a creative bent. It may be in the form of art or music, crafts or teaching, decorating or writing, gardening or friendship. It may even be organizing closets or putting together photo albums. The possibilities are endless. Even those who say they are "not the creative type" truly do have area of talent somewhere (perhaps still waiting to be unearthed). As women, we find enjoyment when we pour out our creative juices and release our talents in specific direction.

The best Mommy Moments may be those spent using your creativity. You can begin by choosing one area you would like rediscover. If you have several creative areas, make a schedule to enjoy different talents throughout the year. Visit a craft or hobby store to gather supplies. You may want to designate one shelf or cupboard to store your hobby materials, or buy a large plastic box for easy storage. Choose certain days during the month which you will work on your projects. This may be a day or a time when the kids go to preschool or during their nap schedule.

Check out craft books and magazines, visit craft shows and attend classes (if you can) to improve your skills and abilities in your special field. Choose projects which have a short duration from start to finish to help you experience an accomplishment. Working together with a friend can bring an added enjoyment to your craft time. You will find it is therapeutic to allow yourself the opportunity to pour your creative talents into a project.

"Creativity involves taking what you have, where you are, and getting the most out of it." C. Mays

5. Creative Outlet

Personal Notes:

_____

_____

_____

_____

_____

_____

_____

_____

_____

_____

_____

_____

_____

_____

_____

_____

_____

_____

MOMMY Moments

6. Delightful Drinks

The British royalty understood the need for a caffeine boost and mood uplifter in the late afternoon to help them make it through the rest of the day. Afternoon tea is quite a delightful tradition and can be an enjoyable moment for mom. Choose one of your warm drinks or consider a cool afternoon pick up listed below.

a) Herbal Teas - The herbal tea market has risen to great heights in recent years. Health food stores have many remedies and teas available and usually knowledgeable assistants to help you make wise decisions. Even your local grocery store now provides several varieties for you to try.

b) Instant Hot Chocolate Delight - 1 (8 qt.) box of powdered milk, 1 cup of powdered sugar, 1 (6 oz.) jar of Coffee-mate™, 1 (1 lb.) box of Nestle's Quik™. Mix the four ingredients together adding a dash of cinnamon if you like. Store in a sealed container. To make a cup take 1/3 cup of mix and fill the rest of the mug with boiling water.

c) Cold drinks - Perhaps you are in the mood for something cool. Using your favorite juice, you can whip together one of these fun, healthy drinks.

d) Fruit Spritz - Pour half a glass of juice and fill the rest of the glass with a lemon/lime soft drink.

e) Fruit Whip - In a medium sized bowl pour 6 ounces of your favorite juice. Add several spoonful of soft frozen yogurt (you can soften it in the microwave). Mix until blended. Even your kids will enjoy this healthy smooth shake.

6. Delightful Drinks

Personal Notes:

_____

_____

_____

_____

_____

_____

_____

_____

_____

_____

_____

_____

_____

_____

_____

_____

_____

_____

_____

_____

7. Life's Lesson Plans

A mother who struggled with her children's sibling rivalries. A woman battling infertility. A wife with a prominent husband. A widow with a new husband. A sweet mother who lost her son. You can find all of these stories in the greatest book of all, The Bible. As you ramble through life's situations and challenges, there is hope found in God's Word with stories, examples, and verses of encouragement.

As a former teacher, I cringe at the thought of trying to teach a lesson to a class of children without first reading my lesson plans and instructions. As a mother, you are a teacher in the classroom of life. The lesson plans from the Creator himself are available to you. Find your help from the Lesson Book of Life and enjoy the encouragement and wisdom it has to offer.

Explore and discover a Bible translation you like and understand. You can find a wonderful variety of Bibles at your local Christian bookstore, complete with study guides and answers to difficult questions. Pick up a Children's Bible for your kids while you are at the store.

Don't know where to begin? May I suggest the gospel of John for starters, in order to have a better understanding of God's plan for life. Genesis is a colorful book to read filled with love and adventure. Esther, Ruth, Psalms, Proverbs, Philippians and Colossians are other books which are especially helpful to women.

All Scripture is given by inspiration of God, and is profitable for doctrine for reproof, for correction for instruction in righteousness.
II Timothy 3:16

7. Life's Lesson Plans

Personal Notes:

_____

_____

_____

_____

_____

_____

_____

_____

_____

_____

_____

_____

_____

_____

_____

_____

_____

_____

MOMMY Moments

8. Joy Journal

Writing out our thoughts, feelings, frustrations and fears can be wonderful therapy. Keep a journal or blank book and pen available for times of reflection and pouring out your heart, but also to write your blessings. Thoughts may become jumbled and cluttered in your mind, but many times when you write them out you are able to see the whole picture of the situation more clearly. Some people write in a journal faithfully every day, while others find an occasional solace using pen and paper. Incorporate the following areas as you use your journal.

a) Problems - Write out the situation you are facing. Be clear and specific. List the obstacles you face. Now list possible solutions. You will find that many times the answer is right in front of you, but you never saw it before. As you chart out the problem it is almost as if you are chatting with a friend for advice. You know the times when you have told a friend a problem and without a word from her mouth, you figured out the solution just by getting it out of your head and into a form you can see or hear.

b) Prayers - Writing can also give you an opportunity to pour out your heart to God. He loves you and wants to hear your cares and concerns. Your pen can provide an opportunity to scribble out your prayer, when your thoughts seem cluttered. Writing out your prayers also provides a way to see clearly the answer to your requests. Date your prayers so you can return and put the date of the answered prayer whether God says, "Yes, no or wait."

c) Praise and Thanksgiving - Count your blessing, count them one by one. Count your blessings see what God has done! Use your journal as a passage of joy, inscribing the blessings in your life.

8. Joy Journal

Thank God for your children, for your husband, for the situations in which He has placed you. Thank God for the difficulties and what He can do through them. And praise Him. Tell God how wonderful you think He is. Pen your praise on the pages of your journal and reflect upon His greatness and power. You will find your cares seem smaller, your kids seem better and God seems bigger as you record your thoughts in these three areas.

Personal Notes:

_____

_____

_____

_____

_____

_____

_____

_____

_____

_____

_____

9. Nap Time for Mom

Your children's naptime can be one of the best times for you during the day. It comes at a time when your body may be weary and your spirit needs refreshment. Guard your children's naptime since you need it as much as they do. Do not let activities come in the way of this important afternoon routine. Consider this short period of time as your off-duty hours. Inform the kids that you will only be available for major emergencies during this time. The kids should learn to stay in their room to rest or play quietly until naptime is over. Set a time limit on naps so your kids will feel the security of knowing when naptime is finished. Of course with babies it is a little different, as they will inform you of their waking hour. The good news is, they do tend to have longer periods of sleep.

A mother's work is never done, so do not think you will accomplish it all during naptime. Instead, designate a certain period of time for chores and a equal amount of time to renewal.

This can be your time to cherish a good book or to pull out your hobby, craft or creative outlet.

If you are sleep deprived due to a young baby or sick child in the house, you need to use this time to rest and revive your physical strength. Remember, most over-tired moms can have a short fuse when it comes to small stresses and challenges. Be deliberate about getting your rest.

A sign on your door or in the kids hallway may be a helpful signal to protect this time. Use a wooden block or simple poster board. On one side write the words, "Yes it is still nap time!" On the other side write, "Now you may get up."

9. Nap Time for Mom

Decorate both sides accordingly with illustrations. This allows you the relief of not having to answer the question "Can I come out of my room yet?" Another idea is to make a small sign attached to a Popside stick which can fit nicely under the door, so that doors do not need to be opened. As your kids see the importance you place on naptime, they too will begin to respect this time and allow you to enjoy it

Personal Notes:

_____

_____

_____

_____

_____

_____

_____

_____

_____

_____

_____

10. Soak Away Stress

Take me away Calgon©! A good soak can be just what the doctor ordered to calm your nerves, relax your muscles and ease your pain. Truly warm bath can soothe the savage beast, emotionally speaking. It's free and it's not far, it's just hard to find the time. Begin by trying to fit a calming bath into a once a week nighttime routine. Agree with your husband that this is an important priority and talk about how he may help with the kids while you soak. You may choose a time after the kids are in bed. Your special soak hour will give you something to look forward to at the end of a harried day.

Begin a collection of bath beads, oils and bubbles. As you are strolling it at the mall or even grocery shopping you may find specials on soothing bath products which would make a normal bath into one of enjoyment and relaxation.

A warm shower is another good tension reliever. If you seem to carry your tension in your shoulders and arms you will especially benefit from this therapy. Stand with your back to the showerhead allowing the warm water to beat down on the tension areas. Stretch your arm out in front of you and above your head as you your showering. Massage your head with your fingertips as you apply shampoo. Close your eyes, relax, take several deep breaths and enjoy the cleansing experience.

10. Soak Away Stress

Personal Notes:

_____

_____

_____

_____

_____

_____

_____

_____

_____

_____

_____

_____

_____

_____

_____

_____

_____

_____

_____

11. Memory Lane

Pull out the photo albums (or shoeboxes) and relish a stroll down memory lane. The walk will do you good as you reflect on the blessings which God has brought you through. You may enjoy taking in some of these photo memories as you reflect in solitude. There are also blessings in bringing in the kids to let them share in reminiscing. We build a heritage with our kids as we teach them from our past. In the Old Testament, God told the Israelites to tell their children the stories of what God had done for them, reflecting on God's goodness to his people. As you pull out the old videos and pictures, you too can use it as an opportunity to pass on the blessed heritage God has given your family.

Old high school scrapbooks, or college photos can be a fun place to start. Laugh and cry about days gone by. Learn from the mistakes and build on the successes. Look at your children's baby pictures. As mothers it helps to see our precious ones in a fresh light. For instance, in the midst of the terrible twos, it helps to reflect on the joy you experienced when you brought your baby home from the hospital. In the midst of sibling unrest it can be reassuring to see a picture of your children playing together in delightful fashion. You may want to enlarge this picture, frame it and place them in a prominent place where the children can reflect on past harmony!

Certainly we do not want to live in the past, but we can allow a stroll down memory lane remind us of our blessings and help us to continue to mature in the life ahead of us. Take some time to enjoy those wonderful photo memories whether they are in albums or shoeboxes, and don't forget to thank the Lord in the process.

11. Memory Lane

Personal Notes:

_____

_____

_____

_____

_____

_____

_____

_____

_____

_____

_____

_____

_____

_____

_____

_____

_____

_____

_____

12. A Mother's Prayer

"The effectual fervent prayer of a righteous man (or mom) availeth much." - James 5:17

"Pray without ceasing." - The Apostle Paul

As a praying mom, perhaps this poem reflects the desire of your heart. Keep it as a reminder to pray not only for the needs of your family, but your strength as well.

Dear Lord,

Help me to honor you today

In all I do and all I say.

Bless my children, this I pray,

As they sleep and as they play.

Grant me wisdom from above

To train my children in Your love.

May our home be filled with peace,

where love and kindness never cease.

12. A Mother's Prayer

Personal Notes:

_____

_____

_____

_____

_____

_____

_____

_____

_____

_____

_____

_____

_____

_____

_____

_____

_____

_____

_____

_____

_____

_____